BRU TI FIED

Robert Benefiel

Brutified

Published By Poetastard Press

ISBN: 9798572460124

First Edition

Cover & Art Design By
Robert Benefiel

Other Books By **Robert Benefiel**:

1)   *Easy Battles For Lazy Armies (1998)*
2)   *After The First Shot (2011)*
3)   *4th & Hill Is Gone Forever (2011)*
4)   *Poetastard (2012)*
5)   *The Sound Of Typing (2012)*
6)   *Laugh Until The Devil Wakes Up (2013)*
7)   *The Human Heart Weighs Nothing In Empty Space (2013)*
8)   *Vote No For President (2013)*
9)   *No Rooms Left (2013)*
10) *The Sun In Rags (2014)*
11) *Love Is What You Think It Is(2015)*
12) *All Over The Damn Place (2015)*
13) *Everybody Looks Down (2016)*
14) *The Crazy Decide Who's Sane As The Flowers Scream For Spring (2017)*
15) *Smoke Outside With The Rest (2017)*
16) *The Morning Roars Slowly (2017)*
17) *Verbalizing Existence (2017)*
18) *Enduring One's Own Mind (2017)*
19) *Femina Aeterna (2017)*
20) *Give The Word (2018)*
21) *Come Under Fire(2018)*
22) *Falling Apart To A Beautiful Song (2018)*
23) *I Wish You Were Never Born And Other Lullabies My Mother Taught Me (2018)*
24) *Getting The Paper (2018)*
25) *Depression, Bleakness, and Their Beautiful Faces (2019)*
26) *Ear Rent (2019)*
27) *Fill It With Regular (2019)*
28) *Classic Works Of Brutal Honesty (2019)*
29) *Becoming Clear (2020)*
30) *You're Too Smart To Know How Stupid You Are (2020)*
31) *The Burning Easel (2020)*
32) *Skinny Street (2020)*
33) *The Endless Ampersand: Love poems 2017-2018 (2020)*
34) *Brutified (2020)*

Compendiums:

1) *Kill The Bottle And Live A Little: Compendium One (2016)*

2) *The Walls Are My Audience And The Words Play Between My Fingers: Compendium Two (2017)*

3) *Person, Place, Thing: Compendium Three (2018)*

4) *Call It Whatever You Want: Compendium Four (2019)*

5) *Renderings Of Hope, Garbage, And Everything Between: Compendium 5 (2020)*

**To Living
Unapologetically**

Table of Contents

The Animals Run Across The Rooves Without Illusion

Demons Tell The Best Jokes

• • •

Always So Close To Knowing

The Animals Run Across The Rooves Without Illusion

Absolutely The Least Amount Of Facial Recognition Possible

I rose in, came in, through the daisy,
stamping the dirt off my boots,
and left a fingerprint on holiness.
I named it Jordan, after the woman
and not the river. I called it that
because it didn't have to be a man.
the shower of emptiness covered
me. the shower of emptiness did not
entirely define me. it was hot.
when I got out I started to shiver.
I looked at myself like a pigeon.
many pigeons caused me to understand begging
only meant you were staying alive for
the next sucker. but can I be sincere
when I say I've had enough time interpreting
your dreams, loading them like shot guns,
as if they could be right
even when they meant nothing?
the flood paused at the precipice, ready to run
through the valley like a rioter into
a liquor store, the shirt cuffs of Armageddon
unbuttoned, but we're still unable to determine
what it's going to do,
sitting there like jane Austin's unfinished novel,
just living off the fame, the heroes
on strike and time handing out the signs,
doing overtime on the
top of the empire state building
as a lightning rod,
changing all the stars

with my wishes,
and all of the stars influencing me
to change them back again,
to whatever they were,
which I am pretty
sure was
John Doe.

Where To Start

your play
is your play, but even a
one man show involves
the stories of others.
if that disturbs you, stop living
awkwardly. admit this is the air
you're gonna have to breathe,
to share: this air right where you're at-
as imperfect as it may seem-
it is all that's keeping you going.
it's a waste otherwise,
and you should picture it
as if you are throwing teeth
instead of dice, which in turn
seems more like throwing a fit
instead of a gamble.
a human heart is not ready for
more than three dimensions.
a battleship is not built for war,
but peace, until someone pulls the trigger.
free your jails of innocent people.
free your future of plans.
stop trying to kill giants
that won't die.
somebody should be raising children
instead of martyrs.
someone should understand
we all have to answer
for everything.
today you told me
you would never lie.

I laughed so hard I sprained a rib,
then the cemeteries started to spin,
and they spun so hard
I saw my grandmother's life
over a thousand and two times
as she flew around and around
like a ghost story
about someone
nobody knows
anymore,
her smile slashing the
neck of the sky,
marking
the place
to start.

Art Project

I have heard them,
many of them,
almost all of them,
in the morning,
in their bathroom,
in my bathroom,
in our bathroom,
always before I get up,
assembling themselves,
preparing themselves for offices,
for retail counters,
for low positons and high positions,
for me and for other people,
for themselves and other people,
for shipments and
for phone calls,
for desks and math class,
for performances
and for introductions,
for glory, for love,
for honor and dishonor,
for little or nothing,
for everything
and twice that.

I have heard them
every morning
making their little sounds-
of bottles hitting counters,
of pill bottles rattling
and being opened,

of faucets being run,
in the clicks and clacks
of cases, the zippers of bags,
the sounds of little glass
and plastic and metal things
hitting each other while other things
were being routed through,
answers being looked for,
colors being looked for,
self examinations being done
in the head of the self ,
the results spread across the mirror,
plinks of little wooden pencils being dropped
and tiny heavy bags being gone through,
of metal tweezers being dropped
and cursed at,
of drawers being opened and
and deep breaths being taken
and rings being taken off and
and pauses, long pauses,
the slowness of lipstick
being applied,
the pucker of lips
as lipstick was applied,
the faces made at themselves,
the brushes nearly silently sweeping
their eyelids and cheeks,
always in the morning,
creating this artwork,
having taken anywhere from
a half hour to an hour,
as I walk past them
and get in the shower,

and already I am
half way done.

then later at night they reverse it,
every night taking themselves apart,
taking themselves
down like a circus,
like oil derricks,
breaking things up,
sending everything home,
leaving a face
showing all its age
and marks,
its moles and zits,
its scars and plainness
and its weight,
its reasons
and reasonlessness.

I always on the other side
waiting until that
door quickly squeaks open,
that hollow door
opening so fast,
seeing the reality
only so briefly before
the click of the light,
the dark of the room,
as whomever
they say they are
gets back into bed,

their lies

no better than
our lies,

and none of us sure
why we do
what we do

even when
it makes
us look
good

sitting
alone.

Life Lessons At The Butcher Shop

Henry's meat shop
was a good place to say
you didn't need binoculars
to get a glimpse
at a real damn tough life,
whether you were looking
at Henry or the cutlets he was chopping,
as his clients watched him tenderize
their selections and talk as loud
as waves in children's ears,
never speaking politics, just beliefs,
saying *NEXT* and never the number,
saying *now I've heard it all*, over and over.
he said he didn't personally name it
to make the place sound dirty, but
he always said that with a grin to the guys.
they would get those lamb heads
wrapped and tied in string,
like the damn life of an animal
was a gift, like there wasn't anything
else to do with the damn things.
the old ladies always asking to cut the fat,
the old men always asking for a little bit more.
the kids just watching the
butcher knife enter
the butcher block
like this was the
way it was meant to be,
bones split in half and brains
put in steel bowls with a price tag,
hooves if you need them, or horns.

* * *

the evening come at 3,
everyone eternally hungry,
as not a person who could afford it
walked away empty handed,
and not a person who ate
wouldn't be empty tomorrow.

Ten Minutes Before You

sometimes when I
wake up
in the early morning

and you are still asleep,

your body looks
empty,

splayed in reasonless
position,

and I look at you
the way
a dog
does
at the horizon-

unable to contemplate anything
other than

waiting
for you,

my current master,

to fill reality back up-

to take your
stretching breath-

waiting for
you
to come
home

in all your
perfect
imperfectness-

turning
the door
handle

as quietly as
the opening
of eyes

and the letting
in of light.

Taking Care Of June

bedpan full of ghosts
spilled onto a white floor,
causing September to slip
and fall into me
and say oh my god
it's you, and the laughter,
oh the laughter,
of eternity-

how it sounds
like my older brother

who was such a brilliant
skinny tall shit

that I said the
same thing July
had said to Cummings
when I saw his first
drawing,

which
was-

I can't believe
you did that
with nothing
but a few
lines.

Summation Of The Dream You Had Where I Die

in the dream
I was quoted
as saying-
"collectively,
were it all one finger,
it would be the middle one.

destiny does not exist
outside the ego or after death."

then I apparently drank from their river
and wound up thirstier than ever.

you said you could tell by the look
in my face, as if it were left half open,
unlocked, by accident.

that was followed by my grasping my throat
and collapsing, where I shriveled up into ash
and poofed away.

after you told me of my 'dream death',
I said in real life,
"imagine all the stars are
rocks on fire being hurtled at us from catapults.

consider the end is so nice it will come to us
without even asking."

you said, "what has that got to do with anything?"

I followed that up with,
"did I at least do something great
before that whole part
in the dream where I die?"

you said, "no."

I said, "well I guess I should be thankful
your brain is not all that reality is made of."

you looked at me and said,
"you are strange."

the only thing I could say
about your dream
after that
was

that it sounded more
like a wish.

Note Found Later

my love,

we are so bad
at saying
goodbye.

I hope
that never
changes.

My 17th August

I will
forever
remember
her

in
her
army
surplus
jacket,

with
long dark
hair

as long
as an
epic poem,

walking
carefully
in the
moonlight,

sweater
so clean

I aged
a complete
decade

when
she asked
for
my hand.

Needed Something To Get Better Sleep

I had to see a therapist
to get these pills,
to secure the ropes around my brain,
that kept me from slipping into
an eternal ocean of black.
after a few questions
he seemed to be leaning
towards me maybe taking
nothing at all,
so to keep things going I
told my therapist,
"I've been working on a book..."
"about what?" he asked.
I told him about what,
filled him on the details.
he said, "that sounds interesting
but I think people just wouldn't care."
I said, "then hell, doc,
why bother writing
Romeo & Juliette
or anything else?
I mean in the end
we don't write and read
because we care,
but because someone
in this world can either
convince us to stay
or convince us to leave,
and all we're looking for
is a little push."
"so you think your book has that

kind of a chance?"
"like everything else,
it has a greater chance of doing that
by existing
than by not existing,
no matter what the critics say."
he said, "well, it's your life."
I said, "Jesus, doc,
is this an assisted suicide?"
he laughed.
then he asked if I wanted
to talk about my childhood.
I asked him the same
question.
he blinked a little and asked,
"are you happy?"
and I wondered,
'is he kidding?'
while looking
at the clock
with a half hour
still to go.

Use The Good Sense Good Thoughts Gave You

I want you to hold what
the sunshine shines on, with your own eyes,
like blue fists around a black hole.
I want you to let it hit your hands
like a high five, slap your back,
and tell you congratulations.
I want you to play with it, feel it,
smile as if you've felt it.
I do not want a smile
produced like a nervous spasm
from seeing a stranger as you pass.
I want you to have the heart
of a crazed sun on your face,
rubbed into your skin and hair.
I want you to press your way into it,
the way fingers find all those songs in pianos.
I want you to walk in it, breath it in,
like the smoke in lounges where mothers sang
and fake romance bloomed in dark leaves.
you should feel worthy of it no matter
who you are or what you have done.
be out there, belonging to no one,
decently faithful, not crazy faithful.
use the light enough to remember what I feel like,
to remember me the way you do the sun
on a spring inflicted day,
to remember me as a decent man,
one who has tried,
a flawed but decent man
who has only you for a god,

a god who only wants my love,
who only wants me to walk freely
and talk freely
and handle that freedom
as one would handle a bet
on their own life,
trusting their own talents,
trusting the light
and feeling that light,
feeling it deep down
as a truth that need
never say anything
even close
to sorry.

Gentle Genius

never a harsh taste
from saying your name-

folding birds
out of my sorrows,
the way violins
make gold out of souls.

I took my arrows
to the garbage.

there was nothing
hidden in you.

I did not have to
hunt for meaning.

you are all
the proof
I need
that things
can, and do,
survive.

you simply
don't evaporate.

It'll Take A Little Defeat To Understand

to destroy your life
all you have to do is love.

I do the smiling backstroke through the rubble,
see the sun when the sun isn't there.

let love destroy you.

it's damage is so precious.

I am telling you,

no one alive
can apparently
live without it.

A Realization While Looking At The
Aftermath When Sadness Dissipates

the dry sea
of my face

calming,

the two storms
above it closing.

expressionless,

Saturn walks into
the field.

the field
stands straight for the scythe.

note that fear's only answer
is to do nothing.

if it can happen
it must mean
the almighty allows it,

and that makes
the idea of this broken
promise,

this funeral,

even worse

when the
meaning of life

is turned into
tall grass

just so it
can be cut.

Irony Without Protection

the woman looked shocked
when she was shot
by the gun she'd bought
for protection,

as her three year old
stopped looking for the gum
in her purse
and said *mommy?*

Imagery Shared By Fallen Leaves And Soldiers

the leaves on the ground
frozen like world war II soldiers
that never made it to the panzers,
huddled in that unmistakable
outline of words, spoken
by a vet who didn't exist
anywhere but in my head,
speaking to the image
laid out before us both
in ripped up Rorschach tests,
stating, "I never would
have joined had I known
the other side wasn't just
going to surrender,
that they'd actually been fed the same
damn good for god and country
bullshit as we were-
that stuff will twist your insides.
that stuff will rotten your teeth and brain.
that stuff, it killed all my friends
and their friends, just to prove
what we already all knew-
we all can agree on one thing.
too bad right now
we don't have a working mouth
to tell each other what the hell that is."

Gravel Voice Road

the screams we were. halos snapped
and used for golden horseshoes.
they say everything is fair in fairness,
but we both know that is impossible.
stars are the loneliest things.

it could be the reason I totaled
my automobile of a chance-
drove it right through morality
and wound up flipped
in a ditch made out of my name.

I surely crawled a long way on
broken bones and broken skin-
but I am glad I did.
it proved so many theories wrong.

it was smelling the bakery
that saved me. it was that thing
that made sense, made me find
goodness' pulse, sending bears
back into their caves, that saved me.

it made me realize:
how could what I have done
been a mistake if it saved
my soul?

I am asking you, my shadow-
when did you realize
I actually move you and

not you me?

did I mention the stars
don't even get a shadow?

quit wishing on them.

quit wishing at all.

if you're going to be anything,
be damned and get the whole
thing over with.

be a human being
and dream something
downright
impossible

and believe it-

if not for my sake

then the sake
of the star
that died
to make you-

who turned
themselves
from light
into nothing
but
dark-

exploding
at night

like one
of those
men
that should
have never
been
a
father.

Done Job Hunting For The Day

summer's just a pun when
you're broke and you can't
even afford the free rain,
sitting on a bench with your
zoo stomach rumbling
and your wildness
weakened by the sun.

sitting on a bench
sweating and itching,
both past and future
gone-

recognizing
that insanity looks like
anything or anyone else
when you are strung out on
bad breath and faces
you don't want to look at,
faces that cannot help you
or themselves.
their smiles, poison.
their prayers, useless.

meanwhile the
children fight over
the swings
and cry at the slides
and the mothers
look at their phones,

people walking
dogs like prisoners,
letting them
piss and shit
everywhere
before they haul them
back home-

and the men like me
smoke
and sweat
and look at the world
that other men
are for some reason
fighting over
and for,

which wouldn't
be so bad
if fifty cents
could buy five dollars
worth of
groceries
and
the bathrooms
were clean
and
the sun didn't hate
us
so much.

Clanging

I could not sleep and pale hearts
went through me - I celebrated my own birthday
on the wrong day. the porter carried my bag
ten feet and then told me he just couldn't.
they were too heavy and full of water.
it was so sad even my own senile aunt couldn't help
but make me cookies up in heaven.
I only hope she is not waiting for me to get there
before she eats them…

It's Hard To Say But Not Believe

tonight the ocean might as well be over.

the crucified are really leaning into their work.

if we are represented by anything
it is our absence.

each casket a garbage can
filled with humanities leftover parts.

the gold leaf peeling off
slowly in silence.

everything is naked.

everything is lying.

we do not know what we are anymore-

we do not know who we are anymore-

and for that we are apparently
eternally grateful.

Somebody Needs Something

somebody forgot
to shut the crowd
and lock it.

it's wandering incoherently
through the streets,

yelling something
about wanting heads
and vengeance.

I honestly don't think
it matters whose head
or what type of vengeance.

when have those things
ever mattered to a crowd?

the Molotov cocktails
swim like fireflies, exploding
against tanks and walls.

the barrier line staggers
back and forth as
the tear gas smokes.

nobody can understand anybody.

you suggest we join them.

I suggest going down to the cellar

where they keep the wine

and wait for the damn
thing to pass with
a few bottles of red and the rats.

I say why bother asking
the world to
notice us now
if that will only
get us killed?

I say if you don't like wine
at least you might like dying
even less.

I tell you that I mean
I don't like rats,
but I like rats
better than crowds.

I offer up
that in the dark
you can pretend
I am whoever
you always really wanted
me to be
when you kiss me

the same way
people vote
for what they
were promised

and not
for what they
actually get.

we stand at the top of the stairs.

we hear the crowd.

I unlock the door

go down
three steps

and look at you,

haloed
by a rocking
ceiling
lamp,

still standing
on the top stair

wondering.

Self-induced Limbo

wilted to the spot,
a musical puddle of brains cupped by the skull,
filled with gray swans who have names like
memory, art, depth, perception-
where else can these beasts call this breast home?
trying to make sense of my parable, the train is late
and the shoeshine man is sick. these things have a
way of happening on their own, godless,
momentum independent of want. it makes the walls
the solid that they are. it makes things stand out.
though it was dark, I was a deliberate color, an army
separated behind the lines.
was I sure that was enough? of course not. I'd have
been okay with knowing everything and then just
dying a few seconds later, but we all know that is
never going to happen if I don't have the guts to
work on my hunch about the bird who's cheating on
the sky- and so I am waiting for that train instead.
for it to come down those closed down rusty tracks.
I am waiting for someone who may never come, to
tell me something I used to know, something that's
important out of all the things I need to know most-
after all, what is freedom without joy? it is none of
the achievements you think they are. whisper to me,
come to me with your stinking sailors breath as I
stand here with a pint of blood in my shoes after
fighting off the blues. come to me, yes me, the most
tired human you will ever find not on a deathbed,
and tell me what love is really like. what can I do
but play with imaginary objects, fold chandeliers,
iron our starched souls until then… even Buddha

wished. it didn't make the wind worse. my entire world the size of two fists pressed together, voices breaking arms, the future blamed on kids, J.J.'s pool hall making more money than the bank of America. it all becomes clearer the more pointless it becomes, the dirtier it becomes, the more depraved it becomes. I should reiterate when I awoke from being awake, I realized there was no going back to sleep. there was only the carrying of doves through the dark- it summarized for me that there was only ever going to be a person that was never going to arrive, to tell me something I needed to hear, with train tracks going under my bed to the tunnel behind me. a tunnel that reminded me we are born, but not out of reason.

Pure Gunslinger

begging would only make it worse.

I heard someone
shout hey.

I heard no reply.

all that was left
of them was the
trash on the ground.

ending wouldn't make
it any clearer.

faith itself is gambling.

the whore doesn't do it because
they love you.

you should know this, son,
but I can't teach you.

the worlds' gonna have to do that.

someone who loves you is going
to have to do that.

it's not my sky,
it's not my mountain.

the talons of the truth

plunged deep
into my head
and dragged me
to the door,

but that doesn't mean
I know what is next
or what to do.

hell, I didn't even make up
any of these words.

I had nothing to do with the rules.

everything is borrowed, kid.

everything
is given back
and faced alone.

Flipping Through Stations

the religious preacher on the radio said
he was excited to know
Nebuchadnezzar would be in heaven,
and how he couldn't wait to meet him
and see what he had been up to.

I wondered did the preacher think
people in heaven
have jobs? hobbies?
wives? children?

I wondered
how people could even
stomach the idea
of an eternity
like that,

working
and
chit chatting
and being
afraid to joke.

who would
want an eternity
of more of the same?

I told the radio to tell him
that I am sure Nebuchadnezzar
would just say he's been dead
in his own language,

one that the preacher would not
speak nor understand
though he claimed to know
what was after death
and best in life,

and he would say it
with black eyes
that the stars
swam
backwards
in,
sucked down
into a big
zero,

while the Neanderthals
and dinosaurs
were all
still
wondering
what they
were doing
there.

You Don't Have To Tell Me

a new species of bird
which sounds
like Rachmaninoff
has been discovered.

there is a picture of it.
it is red and black and blue.

Rachmaninoff
didn't have to ask
if he was good.

neither does this bird.

as great as both of them were,
they still didn't stand a chance
of living forever.

which reminds me:
some children will always
laugh at the old
and the homeless.

it doesn't matter
how wrong it is.

take for example
the moon against
the city building's windows,
how it glows like the make-up
of an undressing clown-

that is why the deer which
dies on the freeway tonight
should remind you

no matter how trapped
we are

we are always wild,

and no matter how wild
we are

we are never free,

but when your
love sticks it in me
I'll swear you are
that new species of
Rachmaninoff
I've read about,

not here so much as
to compose

but to destroy
my preconceptions
of what love
and music
are.

Approaching Actual Reality

I could of swore I saw you
hanging out in the searchlight.
there were reasons you were
in a circle, a gentle villain
wasted on smiles in the
bathroom- the senate had
adjourned, there were laws left stranded
out in the middle of nowhere.
the bad pope had taken off for rome,
the good one stayed at the hotel.
the bear rug tried to put back on a bear,
the moon took off the earth's shade-
it wasn't a coincidence. it was all those lives
just living themselves. I wouldn't apologize either.
if I were to bury my love for you, anywhere,
you know it would be
right here where it started.
I'd write a check to the foundation
of losers, kick up my feet and let
the vultures come on down. I would give up
like a contestant on a game show.
I'd view the view out of the window
as only part of the story-
a spider would climb over another spider if
it had to. I don't see why it wouldn't want
to live like the rest of us, even us
with a lack of money and a form we
don't even know how to fill in-
I brought that up because
I just wanted to get out of these metal boots.
maybe remember how I could hope.

I've been sitting here letting it reappear,
trying my hardest not to stop it.
the best part of my amnesia fading
being when I remembered
what you meant again, walking down
5th avenue with a mouth for a guitar
playing without lessons
or the common sense
to know when to stop.
watching you dance,
it freed me.

Put It To Bed

if we can't have
any good days we might as
well grow fond of the bad ones,
some eternities being longer than others.
the way the razor comes at us
promising either a shave or a slit throat.
my marbles tossed into the air
just to see the effects.
I wanted to call the nurse,
I wanted something
other than ambivalence
to pay attention.
each ghost crowding my guts
like a gas chamber;
still I cannot pull the switch,
I cannot kill them.
they are my only friends.
and if they go…
if they go…
I fear I may never
know the truth again.
I fear I will never
be wanted again,
except by all the empty
wine bottles still looking
for me, having had me end
their lives so happily
it would disgust mister
Satan himself,
still standing there
waiting for a pour.

The Old West In Me

inspiration,
come be a stab wound in me.
intensify into a fortune.

the swagger of my blood
as it staggers through my veins,
stumbling over words
that never got out of me.
my eyes can only speak to the one I love.
I hope you can understand me.

I cannot do my moon over.
I cannot repeat my tomb.
I've reached my ash point, declined into
red tide, then risen into steam –

I was a good man nobody wanted.
I was a horrible man everyone needed.

that's my whole speech dear.
seriously, that is it. now
I plan to go to the future
field in which the honeysuckle
monsters sway, and read it out loud.

I want the last thing
I say to be as close to yes as possible.

I hope they can understand me.

Work Sick

shaving my teeth before bed,
removing the diamonds from my eyes-

if nails can hold up the son of god
I certainly hope
they can hold up this old place
another day,
darling.

I hope I have
another day, darling.

the way things are going
I wouldn't be surprised
if all of our breathing
was being run by Edison/Pacific
as I splash acid across my face
just to get the look off of it.

does that answer how things are going?
does that answer how my day was?
no?
        ...well, they were so low
on men to berate and destroy this morning,
that I went in healthy and came out sick.

sick of work, sick of what it gives me.
the exchange of money for body
not feeling even, even if it's considered more
than what most humans get.

it turned out I even took some devil thought
away from its owner today,
just put it in my head like a bag lunch
and carried it around, then I let it loose
outside like a bird, like I said
with each cough, "go be good evil,
go be good…"

for if I am looking for a favor
I'm not looking hard enough.
my coffin needs no pillows,
a cave is a church, a church is just a building,
and that doesn't mean I want to go to church,
dear elephants wandering a place I will never go,
traipsing through the wasteland
carrying sugar to an already dead king,

I have no idea why man is an animal
that can only think of itself
no matter what it is thinking
(notice the women think their different)-

perhaps it's the sugar's fault, who knows-
regret is a word the fresh fires cannot burn
but guilt is its own knife to the throat,
the moon always saying *join me!*

whether it's the guy with his mouth stuck open
in the dentist's chair or the woman
in a noose speaking her mind,

the horses in the 7th already know
the outcome of the race.

the universe, my friend,
already doesn't care.

our mind having had to fast
all 7 days,

dead but still alive-

I am so tired
I sound like
an angel,

and after having
fucked
Eloise for
two hours

it's no wonder
I need
to trim
my nails-

though the
medal of honor
afterwards
was a surprise.

Demons Tell
The Best Jokes

One Tragedy At A Time

Euripides blood running like a river
from the mountains of his chest;
some cannot appreciate a better man
than themselves. take solace that
fate is crueler than chance.
choice is the only illusion we have.
now even Euripides knows that.
take two sugars, take a life,
call me a nation in the morning
and strip me of my visa.
the tea boils on a dead man's stove,
his hands clutching his crotch,
the officers saying he tried to fuck
his tea kettle. I don't want to know
what drives a man to try that. most
don't deserve a pyramid, not even some of
the pharaohs, but I deserve better
than a trash can. I deserve more than
a tea kettle to sleep with. I deserve
more than police officers standing
over me wanting to take a shot.
syrupy light, oozing over
plants stuck in bowls.
the blue balled devil
running out of options
as the bar closes.
they who need always need more.
they who bleed know they bleed.
got a spare tire but no car.
got a life but nowhere to live.
had what I thought was a heaven

until I realized no one would fit in it.
perhaps it's best not to second guess death.
it said do not dig for bones in moving flesh.
now that you are young and beautiful, in words,
I must accept if the concept of ice is permanent
then it is me who melts.

Predator Perched Down Wind

like me, owl, offer me fine mice,
or don't. be true to the things that kept you alive.
I howl non-Ginsbergian (you cannot keep
that word any more than Walt can own yawp)
the emotion we brag about inside a candy bowl:
there is no such thing as cold
right now, arm swimming wide ways,
to the top of my own tree,
reverent of paths not ever cut open before,
the wild cat in the corvette
growing fatter and dumber
by the mile.
hesitant to say this is the way to peace,
let alone happiness, like a youth with
a pocketful of used cigarettes
because they can't afford any,
splitting open what
I would say is the first layer,
separating the fruit from its skin,
a chest full of first place trophies
hidden in shame.
a simple life cannot be a full life,
you cannot call
what you do a choice,
until you
return the drink to
the woman at the bar,
turning down not only her
mice but your execution,
as she asks with her face
from afar

what history asks,
and the owl asks,
and the orphan
asks,
and the knock
knock
joke asks,
continually,
with and
without question-

who.

who.

who.

Wandering Through The Court

your dead thoughts
dipped in dripping butter,
making a crunching noise
in an eternally chewing mouth,
having went from net to plate just like that,

the idea made stupid
before it was ever listened to,

as flowers have no king
and invade the hillside,

all of us with a drinking problem
of one kind or another
(not enough water, not enough whiskey)-

our Sunday tipped over
and spilled in patterns
created by chance,
that upon viewing has
riddled our flesh with sense
while our minds cannot believe it,
the ram having taken the hill
now leaving-

incompetence is found
easiest by throne,

and I will stand,
I will stand here,
bored

(I was so obvious
as a ram-

much more
than I was
as a poem).

Santa Monica Mall

I'd just started
going down the escalator,
leaving my job
after a long day
in the stock room,
when I heard someone
calling out

THERE HE GOES!

I turned towards the voices
and saw a young midget being
chased by a bunch of kids,
and they were all running my way.

the boys chasing the midget
were obviously much larger
than the midget, and

from where I stood
it looked like a simple act
of irrational savagery,

but the midget,
god bless him,
still had good speed,
and he was weaving
and bobbing
between people
with ease.

sadly it was probably not his
first or last time being chased,
cruelty does not know when to quit,
and so I watched as if I were a director
with no say in my own movie,

as he kept getting closer
and closer
while the escalator
kept taking me down

until my eyesight
was level with his eyesight.

the look
of terror in his eyes

as he got closer to the steps

was solid,
like a mastodon,

and I could hear
the boys chasing him too.

I could hear them so well
it was like I could see them too,

their bodies possessed with
absurdity
as they mangled
space on
their way

towards us,

with the last
stretch between
the escalator and him
suddenly becoming
this short straight shot.

it seemed tough
that the midget had realized this
way too late,
this burst of energy
over taking him,

and as he got closer
to the escalator
he must have realized
he was going
far too fast to stop,

for I watched
his eyes grow
as he yelled out
OH SHIT!
before he could
slow down-

and that is where
the moment turned from horrific
to magical-

for even though
he didn't stop in time

he flew into the air
about a foot over my
hunched body,

and he flipped while
doing so,

then landed
almost perfectly
on his feet

8 steps after me.

if there had been
judges there
they would've given
him straight tens.

after he landed
he turned around and
looked at me,
then he looked
back down the escalator,
then again back at me,

as if to ask me,
with only the look on his face,
if that really happened-

but after he saw
the boys standing
at the top of the electric stairs

standing still and silent
over my shoulder,

he saw that they couldn't
believe the magic either.

in fact no one could believe it,
and they were there.

every one of us was silent
and observant of that
which we could
not know.

it was as if the gods for some
reason had chosen that moment
in that place to prove they somehow
were there.

while the midget boy stood there in shock
security came up behind
the other boys at the top of the escalator,

but the boys at the top scattered
and ran off as
the security tried to grab
at their shirts and hair and arms.

meanwhile,
on the other end,
when the midget got to the bottom,
security was also there

and they pulled him aside,
surrounding him by hot dog on a stick.

they started to talk to him
as if this were somehow his fault.

I got off the escalator
and I started walking off,

but I didn't really want to walk off.

I wanted to tell the midget
he was incredible,
and that if that unplanned stunt
wasn't proof of that
I didn't know what was.

but they just escorted
the midget off
before I could say anything,
whisked him away
through some private door,

as it seemed like
nobody knew what
to do when something
good happened,

because they
just hadn't seen it
before.

Longs Or Shorts

clerk, standing beneath a cloud
of cigarette boxes, looking up
as if he were looking up into death
for that right flavor, bringing the box
down and handing it to a kid
who has no idea, just cash.

Renting Out Near The Cape

we were standing in line
waiting for food.

the waitress came out and
told a young man
his mojo fries would
be ready in a minute.

he replied he had been waiting 20 minutes
just for mojo french fries.

I was waiting for tacos.

I had been there maybe for
three minutes.

after a minute or two,
the young man turned
to me and he said
in a thick rural accent,

"I have been waiting for my mojo fries
for 20 minutes, sir."

I'd heard him tell the counter lady
that same thing.
it seemed like all he wanted
was someone to understand his life.

I said, "oh yeah?"

he said, "yes sir."

I almost made a comment about
the sir thing, but he seemed nice enough.

his face was covered in soot,
and he wore blue coveralls.

I said, "where do you work?"

he said, "the refinery, sir."

I said, "how do you like it?"

he said "I have never held a grinder
for 8 hours a day. my arms feel like
concrete noodles."

I said, "sounds rough.
how long have you been there?"

he said, "three weeks."

I said, "how you liking it after three weeks?"

he said, "I like the pay.
I'm saving for a house
and at least I can get beer on the weekend."

the lady came up with
a bag and looked at me
and said, "here you go."

I smiled and took the bag.

the young man said,
"where are my mojo's
ma'mm?"

she said, "they are coming.
they have like 30 seconds more."

on my way out
he said, "have a good night sir
with his heavy drawl."

I said, "don't let
the day close on a bad note.
get them fries."

he said, "will do sir."

I got out to my
car, started it, and
felt bad for that kid,
who liked drinking
beer on the weekend
and saving money for a house
he was never going to own.

they got a hold of him
before reality could,
before it could tell
him there were other
places he could go.

I left him still
standing there
in the window
waiting
for fried potatoes.

fried potatoes, for Christ's sake.

the world was always going to make
that man wait for something, I thought.

then I drove off
and saw the row of street lights
leading me back to sheriff road,

making my way back
to the rental,

no different than anyone else

who gets hungry for
a living.

Asleep Before You Got Home

flesh being
the clothing of life-
do not get undressed
my Lydia.
you're much better
at beauty
than bones,
for what I sear into my navel,
into my center,
is not iconoclastic mockery.
even if my emotions are the shambles,
my feelings of you are intact.
they are how your movements
spice the lesson of control,
make titular thoughts
appear, and stain history.
it made me so tired to love you today
that my eyelids have already dropped,
my eyes trapped and dry,
making them itch until I scratched
them wet and released ideas
like wild dogs into dreams.
so while this happens and I cannot talk,
but instead only breathe,
I point without hands at the invisible letter
in your breast that I wrote for you.
I ask you to sustain your voice with apple,
recognize the hint of gold
in a sky we do not control-
I know I sleep in a stabbed night
as harsh as cold dead stone,

as harsh as a nice murderer's eyes,
as harsh as concealed poison dressed in wine,
but understand the tunnel to the city
makes things like reason disappear,
and tonight is no different-
the soul simultaneously
sheared of its afflictions and visibility-
but please wait here for me to wake up.
wait for me to reappear in life.
let me join you and listen to you.
you can teach me love
and I can show you how that helped
through the description I wrote
of what really happened on my journey down,
the hounds scattering into the light
after finding no colors to hate.
let me explain that we are not lost,
while the days drop things
like coins and babies,
as they run
from our
honesty and arms.

Compressed

having gotten so close, we crush the ends of
sunshine between us, making them solicit
otherverses, otherwheres, similar to those of
so what if god doesn't like me?
the orchestra trying to play and run
at the same time-
what a little darling chaos can be sometimes...
brought fresh nectar in the morning-
a weird sense of almost polarizing
choices, of whether to enjoy
the color grass or the inner lip
or the knife sunbathing on a napkin-
as if any of this had to make sense.
christ, love is often
better when it doesn't.

Groggy

how can I not shout
in my sleep and
feel red when
the tossed over tables
lay in their thrown up coins,
the electric fan
with a bent blade
tickling away at its own ribs
as it chews on the hollow air,
how it keeps cutting it up
with its jaws and
spitting it out cold,
the last patch job already
peeling off the
patch job before that,
the bare wires of
death smiling,
the only thing left
of simplicity
being the admission
that one does not know,
nor will ever fully know,
each head crammed with
some version
that just won't fit
in someone else's head
no matter how much
you beat it,
the woman of our dreams
leaving our head
and slamming shut the eyes,

the only trusted star
wished upon
in the sky
pointing at us,
saying that even if you
get your wish of never dying
death is still coming
after your loved ones
who do.

An Old Tibetan Saying I Came Up With Last Week

those who
sleep easily
at night

have forgotten
the world
they sleep in.

For Your Service And Allegiance

there were F18's overhead,
saw a bald eagle,
a van had a knife spray painted on its side
that looked like it were ripping it open,
a woman stood up in a bikini top
flashed me and screamed yahoo,
and for a second even I thought
I might be patriotic.

I dropped my girlfriend
off and said I would
meet her at the entrance,
the sound of marching bands
playing over megaphones,

but as I was driving around
looking for a place to put the car
I was stopped behind a man
honking at another man in the parking lot
after he swooped in
and took the spot the other man
had already been waiting for.

immediately they began yelling
out their windows at each other
about this parking spot,
how the ones not in the spot
had been there first,
but the ones in the spot
said they were too slow,

and even though
there were plenty of other spots
still to be had all around them,

they stood everyone up
yelling at each other,

until the yelling
turned into the families
getting out of their cars,
pointing and threatening each other,
until finally the two families
came together in a mesh of
fist throwing and
kicking at each other.

even the little ones were fighting each other.

I sat there watching this from my car
until I decided even the fall of mankind
can be boring, and honked.

this stopped them
just long enough for me
to drive around
the whole thing,

and I found a spot
not two places over,
parked,
and then walked back
past the commotion
still going on.

by this point two little girls
were pulling on each other's hair.
one woman had another woman
in a choke hold while a boy
stood there pointing at them and crying.
of course the real piece da resistance
were the men who had started
the whole thing, dancing around
to the sound of a bad country song
playing from one of the cars,
grabbing at each other like guys
who took wrestling in high school
and exposing their fat white bellies
as they took swings that missed
by a mile.

I felt bad most of all for the underpaid
security guard yelling at them to stop,
he not understanding they wouldn't stop
while the other people, their fellow countrymen,
were whooping and egging them on.

America, I muttered under my breath as I went past.

I wondered at that point if Spain
might be a better fit for me, if not us all,

wandering towards the stands
to look for the woman who dragged me here

and whose future was honestly
never really going to be with me.

Everywhere Are People Dying And That Alone Doesn't Make Them Special

many people, in places such as
down the street or where you work,
are dealing with failing body parts,
aging, memories going, marriages ending,
bills that won't stop coming
and money that never stops leaving.

there are many sitting in
your waiting rooms severely depressed,
and whether you did anything or not,
they will take whatever gripe they have
out on you.

throw in a learning curve,
police who may not care, mayors with
a drinking problem, dirty water,
lonely landlords,
and you start to understand
the depths and darkness of the idea
that no matter how well
you light a dungeon
it is still a dungeon.

it's like when people
brag about working at a county jail.

sure they may get a decent check,
vacations and sick pay,
get to go home Friday,
etc.

etc.,
but they still
have to come back to jail
on Monday morning,
willingly.

once you realize that
you may understand
why I toast those at my table
by saying yatzhee.

we will not always win,

but goddamn it,

we should at least
enjoy losing.

It's So Important I Just Don't Care

the stove
wears the flame
crown,

and I struggle to find
happy thoughts
bigger than this.

each vein assigned
the hopeless task

of sending blood
to the right parts,

as I am for some reason
enamored
with the white tiles

that seem to be
both outside of me
and inside of me

whenever I look
at something.

my brain
down to
one
little
lost boson
that is

somehow
still pure,

watching
the water
boil as if
I'd finally
found insanity
more peaceful.

When Did I Know I Could Write

decades ago, I felt an idea come in from under the
bed, tried to kill it with a shoe, but it went straight
for my eyes, and it got in. I was fucking infected,
but unable to afford a doctor. I was just a kid,
really, but somehow I don't think that mattered.
so I rode the idea out, through bad sleeps and
laughter, jotting down whatever it commanded me
to write, my brain kicked open like a door and
my soul hanging out like an untucked shirt,
and maybe what I thought no one should have to
think for as long as I thought it, but I felt like I had
no choice and that giving into it was all I could do,
and when it was all over, maybe I should have felt
used, but instead I felt whole and alive, better than
ever, so I gave in for years, thought after thought,
until one day I looked around and realized my mind
just up and left with no forwarding address. there
were other things missing too. it had left me with
bills, an addiction, gouged out my soul, swiped my
money, took the tea pot, and let my cat escape. the
fact that may car was still there was the only good
part. that's when I said good riddance, packed, and
went and looked for my next idea, and when I found
that I looked for my next, and I just kept looking
and I just kept going, until finally arriving at an
apartment in Oregon and picking up a woman's bra
off the ground, I realized I had been typing for over
50 years, and to celebrate I pulled down the blinds,
and got on with it, for however much longer it
would last, which from the looks of things was too
long, since it kept going on even after my death.

The Bad News Is The Good News

the bad news is I have gone insane. the good news
is it's better than being sane. I think of a cigarette
burning, loved ones missing me so much they try
and dig me out of the ground with their bare hands.
neither is really happening. I am doing this to keep
my mind off of someone. someone I love so much
that I don't know how to love them right now. have
you ever loved someone like that? like you loved
them so much it made you feel bad for loving them?
like you ruined something and you don't know
how? I am so crazy I don't even know if I am
asking you, or myself, or the person I imagine
reading this with their own voice, when I ask that.
the only thing I can be thankful for is that I am
insane right now. maybe it is only temporary,
just as all things are temporary. no one can be
happy forever. no one can love all the time.
eventually even the rich can't make any more
money. those ideas seem just as insane. of course it
can't be any saner to think that there is no such
thing as love, that there can be no such thing as
forever. maybe I have been tricked into believing
whatever I believe is wrong. maybe I have trusted
the wrong ghost, the wrong imagination. maybe I
am defective. maybe the others are broken. who can
tell the broken they are broken if they do not believe
they are broken, if the healthy have been convinced
they are sick and the sick told they are healthy. trust
is so easily broken. people are so easily broken, and
yet we try to act so sane. when is an action taken
that it isn't considered selfish. I don't think anyone

can refrain from being manipulated, but how do we know they weren't manipulated by someone else? I don't think I know, but maybe I do and I have been fooled into thinking I don't. I guess that means I am trying to act sane by thinking. I am not stuck in traffic, but I imagine myself to be. while I am stuck in this imaginary traffic the cars on the other side move quickly like they do in real life. then I turn my head to the left and look at the white wall. it is an old habit of mine. I imagine myself saying something that will make you love me longer than a day. I imagine you saying something that will break open the universe like a sugar cane bone and let me suck it out. like I said, I am a little crazy right now. like I said, that might be the good news.

This Can't Be Pointed Out On A Map

my advice- go west forever.
hide in a match.
hitch a ride on an idea-
not this one. this one is mine. it carries
no dead weight. it rejects orders.
you need your own, trust me.
you will want to name it. me-
I carry large barrels of water,
flour, eggs and apples, through
the expanse.
I bring enough to barely last as a fool.
but I still know why I left.
I still know it goes sea-forest-mountains-grassland-
              plains-mountains-sea.
I know it goes dirt-mud-rock-water-ice.
I know it goes paths-roads-highways-tunnels-rails-
              airports-launch pads.
I don't need to know my destination, how I die.
I have other reasons to move.
one needs a reason to move.
movement without motivation
is emptiness in action.
you do not need to invite anyone.
you can go it alone.
you are already a stranger
everywhere you go.
you should still learn how to speak the language.
you should still say something.
love something. learn how to think.
most only learn by fear.
you should try something different,

like hating something you don't know
until you don't hate it anymore.
you should go west, forever.
you'll like it there.
it might in fact
be the only place
you like.

Teamed Up For A Bit

she had a dress
made of old dust rags,
and when she danced
she really cleaned the place up,
and I thought love would come for me
but it was a no show.
so instead I looked
at the little pocket map
I had. I realized where I
wanted to go was not
on any map. Instead
I lit it with the table candle.
the bartender came out from around the bar
and asked if I was crazy.
I placed my switchblade on the table
and said should we find out?
he backed up as I stood up,
and then I walked towards
the door, the map still burning.
I heard him talking on the phone
to the cops, but I didn't care.
I knew if I just chose an alley
no one saw me enter
I would be fine.
when I reached the door
the woman with the dust
rag dress asked
can I come along?
I said you know nothing
good can come from this.
she said that isn't

why I'm asking and
that isn't what I'm looking for.
I nodded towards the exit
to one more existence.
I opened it for her.
the door closed purposely.
we went down an alley,
leaving the sirens
and flames
behind us
the old fashioned way:
guiltless.

Through Here To Strange

I took carpenter street
because it was faster than
darrow boulevard
that day,
and I did the usual jump across
the big lane, took the smaller left
feeling like I had not left
the world but was still
satisfied with it,
it just didn't seem against me,
the road was that clear,
and then I parked
on the street, because the
street parking was free
but the parking lot was not,
but I was so early
I still had a half hour to kill,
and I was good at murdering time,
just ask my ex,
and so I decided to take a little walk,
just enjoy some blue air
and not having to be somewhere yet,
and as I walked along
I was looking up, because something
went into a tree, or came out of a tree,
but something made the leaves move,
and that is when I heard a voice say
HEY,
and I looked down,
and I was inches from almost stepping on
a lady, a lady just laying there on the sidewalk,

her head propped up by her hand,
laying there on the concrete like she were at
central park watching a concert that was no
longer there, and I looked at her the way you
would look at someone who is where you
don't expect them to be,
and I said you need any help?
she grimaced.
do you? she asked.
I said
I guess crazy day
is being celebrated
early
this year,
and I walked off,
as she continued to look
at her phone like it
was finally
going to do
something,

all of us, nothing
but murderers.

How Enemies Work After The Battle Is Over

the battle now over-

the enemy tanks
start to roll in,

their turrets shoved into
the skies back,
pushing towards
the center of town.

the soldiers fought.
the soldiers died.

the only difference is one
side lost more men than the other.

now those men,
those soldiers
who won,
apparently can
tell those who didn't win
what to do,

no matter how
absurd the request-

and so they march,
over the dead and destroyed,
to get to the last seven whores
seemingly left
on their side of the

entire world.

it is as much sense
as the world can muster

while the tanks
and boots crunch through
the disassembled streets,

only to be
jolted awake
by a young and optimistic man
jumping out of nowhere,
standing before
the tanks,
trying to stall them,
waving
a sword and screaming
that they will not win.

notice he did not
try to liberate the whores
first. notice the whores
didn't ask to be liberated either.

a loud crack is heard
and he slumps
to the ground.

the colt cools
in the lap of the town sheriff
as he waves the enemy tanks
and soldiers in.

the children salute
the enemy as they go by.

their parents continue
to pick through the rubble
and resentment,
handing over
their cans of food, blankets,
and young men.

and the tanks roll right on through,
towards the center of town,
over the heads
of those who thought
they'd get something
for complying or
surrendering
or dying,

the joke
going on and
on,
towards
the center
of town

as the afternoon
hits their backs,

as everyone
burying their
dead and digging

up their jewelry
starts to understand,

that just
by observation

it looks like
the amount of
whores in town
just went up.

What Room Am I In?

the days become rooms,
always aging.

the days become rooms,
multiples and multiples of rooms,
strung out and used.

the days become rooms,
the same way people
become stories,
and I have no idea
who you are now
and where
I am waking up today.

a spare room, a rubber room, a bathroom?
how about a torture room
or a pool room?
how about a holding room
or a book room?
will it be a back room
or lead to a back room?

will I be able to breathe there-
leave there-
dance there
or speak there?

will there be others in the room
or just me?

will it allow me to be happy,
force me to be sad,
or hang a poster up of me
to stare back at me?

will it encourage me to be upset,
angry, ready to thrust a torch
through the white house window?

will it allow me to preserve my thoughts,
grow my plants at night, or allow a novice to
look through the microscope upon my cells?

will I have to rent the bed that is there
or sleep on the couch?

will it have a sink? refrigerator?
handcuffs through the bed board?

can I write letters there
or read them?

will ghosts demand I leave or stay?

will it have blood on the floor,
or on the ceiling, or under the rug?

will it have other stains on the bed,
crumbs around the stove, the Sunday comics
stuffed under the floorboards?

will someone
be looking through a window,

turning a locked handle,
or saying not to come in because they're naked?

will there be someone telling me what to do
for 8 hours, or wine on the table?

will there be a knife,
a picture of someone I do not know,
a biblical saying that says nothing
hanging over a desk?

how about a loud clock
or a safe or a tv turned to the wall?

will it have a view of a revolution,
will it have a wall missing due to the bombing?

will a woman holding a bleeding child
wail down below? will a bird fly through the
roof? will I find mushrooms where I shouldn't?

will a woman be in my room hitting me
with her hands or will she be just a name carved
into the water heater?

will there be fish lined up on ice, apples,
people who speak something completely different,
know more than I, or less?

will there ever be a room where someone else there
doesn't know more than I?

will the shadow of a demon appear

at two in the morning after passing
though a certain branch
at a certain time of the year?

will a train run by,
a man shout damn you,
in the distance?

will a person with a gun
come in
and start blasting the place?

will some music be playing?
will someone be waiting for me?
candles on a table, and a note?

what if it were one where
I was getting kicked out of it?

what if it's a place I can fix my car?

what if I can get my eyes checked,
my heart inflated, and
my mind crutches?

the possibilities
wearing a red that is
either blood or
wine-

I had my mind
when I came in, but

who knows,

who knows.

the days are rooms-

the days are rooms-

the days are always rooms-

that once left
are locked

and remain that way.

This Time With A Little Less Piss
And A Little More Pizzazz

erased down to the heart.
the hate of a woman lodged
into my side like an axe into a barrel.
the windows so very high.
apparently my soul
can be folded like a flag
and put away.
there are other parts of me
that cannot stop being what they are.
when my soul isn't there
this is what you get:
a day from long ago. an unfinished lesson.
I have no idea what my parents
emptied into me while I slept.
I'd wake and something felt off.
I have no idea what I am really
responsible for.
the deer, the one that makes you
go aww? it hasn't been seen in some time.
no one has said anything.
it can feel as awkward as suicide to speak of it.
I know this as well as you know yourself.
I know this because
I always get mistaken for a soldier.
I always get a rifle put in my hands.
people like to fight me, like to watch me fight.
they like to forget.
since no one asks to be born
it makes sense, but in the weirdest of ways
I feel like I would have asked anyway.

I have never sailed but I have read how to sail.
I do not think that would save a single ship.
I open my pockets and nothing goes in or out.
I open my eyes and nothing
goes in or out. there is a constant
that believes nothing else.
the only thing I can tell
is that the orchestra
is not what you think
and apparently every single
living child still eats,
and apparently not every
single living child
gets something to eat.
this does not bother
some people.
they just go aww
like they do when the
deer's eaten from the branch.
as a last ditch effort
all I can say is
please, whatever
powerful thing you are,
give me dawn.
a large dawn.
feed me
something
that won't kill me.
feed the children
something other
than neurosis.
draw me back
into existence.

open my eyes
with that crowbar
called faith
and don't
just stand there.
give me purpose,
not excuses.

Old Magicians Trick Using Greed And Sleight Of Hand

elections surrounded by barbwire
with arms and pleads sticking out of them.

you cannot force a tragedy
to behave differently.

everyone lost their mother today.

note the way the sun hangs crooked.

note the way idiots believe anything.

guilty is a decision, not a part of nature,
and I know your eyes.

they've been trained by love
to hurt people.

the rumor is my government flips coins.

it's not a rumor.

it's a lie.

they wouldn't spend that much money.

everyone knows why they do what they do.

look at those coins.

just look at those coins.

never mind the graves-

just look at what happens
to the coins.

Doesn't Matter If She Was A Woman

not the way I would imagine a daisy to grow,
so giant it needs its own place and has to work
to pay the bills, but man, the crooked old men
really worked hard to miss this one, the way
she made a dancer blush, hushed me with a finger,
then emptied all those boxes at burden's feet,
and said, "take 'em, you stupid son of a bitch.
what good do you think trying to
rebuild me out of garbage will do anybody…";
I mean who else could hold up a train
as good as the bridge bandits who never
came back from Mexico? I swear the prairie's
flat just because it would be scared to trip her,
because if the mountains are a jury
I am pretty sure it was unanimous
that they let her go, because some experiences
are better experienced
by everyone than just alone:

everyone can read a poem,
or have it read to them, buddy,
but few, few can be one.

Painting Titled The Mistake

I went in looking for
a cheap toothbrush holder
when I ran across
one of my own paintings in
this second hand store.

it was hanging on a wall
next to a coo coo clock
and a beer sign.

I had given it to a woman
who said she could not
live without it.

apparently she lied,
or she was dead,

but I doubt she'd died,
though who knows.

either way, at this point,
she was a bit dead
to me.

while standing there and
seeing my stuff on the wall
it made me wonder
if any other artists had run
across their own work
like this.

if they had just walked over to a garage sale
to look at the ties and there was one of
their works standing in the sun,
next to a bag of rags, a stroller,
and an incomplete set of golf clubs.

I walked up to the counter.
and asked, how much for the picture?
10 bucks, they said.
really? can't go any lower?
7.50 is as low as I go.
deal.
he took it off the wall.

I've had that thing hanging up
there for so long I forgot it was there, he said.

some things just wait for us
until we find them, I said.

I took my little painting home.

I sat it on the couch,
then sat down on the chair
across from it.

I looked at it.
and looked at it.
and looked at it.

I wished I could have
apologized to it,
but sat back instead.

my new lady came home
from work and saw
the painting.

what the hell's that?
she asked.

a painting, I said.

of what?

what does it look like?

a mistake.

I said,
you nailed it.

Defending Against Invisible Specters In Exaltation

it is like this
in places you dream are good:
the curve of the fire resting thin and little,
strips of light painted on our vulnerability,
made massively Matisse and plump
while retaining the edges.
moon hung out like a Halloween decoration,
the night making heroes of us,
solving war in our embrace.
this fasting that has ended
as I consume you,
as if I were the rain, and the
rain actually cared.

Still Gonna Give It Another Shot

I am dog plastered across the road, final
about my decision- to shout into the steel pot
at its refusing to fill is worthless-
roll your strangers and get yourself
both the karma you need and don't,
walk down those streets that used to have
porno theaters,
entertainment that was replaced
with even worse mediums.
just look and see the same things
you saw before-
a couple of generations
that can't get out of nostalgia,
stuck like a fat man in a doorway.
the things we're remembering…
meanwhile no one can figure out how
to write their name in cursive.
by far the pigeon has won its right
to shit on anything we build.
the bodies hunching early
to look into computers they call phones
while savior after savior is picked off
to keep the whole thing going.
no rebellion, no equality,
just people thinking this is the way
it's always been,
so it must be the way it has to go-
though I assure you it is not, and it should not
be considered that way- but no matter how much
I bathe in good memories, I get this dirty feeling,
this feeling of being tricked my entire life

over a rumor, over a fantasy,
over a flame that never was,
over a thing that never was.
though it seems too late to be anything
other than drunk or stupid or lost,
maybe even all three at once,
trust me, there is more.
I don't care how much cancer you have.
I won't change my story.
I can't tell you it's all been worth it.
take it from the source:
you do not want my life,
nor its pains, nor its defeats,
nor even its happy moments.
they do not make sense anymore or last.
they do not shine, and they mock my honor,
showing me to be as naïve
as a person who answers an ad for love
only to realize they've actually answered
the ad for divorce.
you want your own life.
you want your own memories instead of mine.
right now instead of watching reruns
I look at the shoes on my feet,
standing there, being there,
where no one and nothing is.
I am trying to think of something
that is not someone who has died
or disappeared.
I am gambling on a chance
that one day things
might make sense,
my last few dollars on the table

as I throw the dice into a hole,
the runner telling me
they will tell me the truth
but only if I lose everything,
which is something
I honestly heard the last time,
but what else is there to do
except pretend
until it really happens.

Punch Line Discovered On The Back Of A Medication Prescription

the joke aspiring to be real enough,
not to be dismissed, a universal truth
that can put a good pollen laugh into the air,
make deities sneeze and devils take some blame,
for I saw my terrible eyes do their best
to see what it was, and I heard
it was more about what it was
that I wasn't seeing. apparently it was
a lot of everything. the geese might have
not come back, but I couldn't lay it
all down to what I said. others have to be
involved in this chaos. others have to be there
when the heart explodes and the crown
of Budweiser shorts out. the west
tromping through the mud with
an armful of old greeting cards,
the kind that wreak of having nothing
to say, just signatures as easily given away
as flirtatious looks. fruit rotting
on the dock is what they call that.
abusive relationships with gods
is what they call that. building hells
before we even get there is
a completely wasted effort. I called
life a forged painting and I think
you know what I mean.
we're never in the right place
until it's too late and we're buried.
until the time itself doesn't believe
what it is saying,

and what I am about to say
instead is a good thing,
this little
thing I picked up
off the ground
in a place outside of
a tungsten steel warehouse,
when I was between
work as a donut cook
and a writer of air,
air that was used to tell
anyone who needs to
to live to go ahead and start,
and it starts
with:

have you ever heard
of the truth?

and
its ends with:

well until you tell it
you
still haven't…

Getting Chilly

seconds turned into heirlooms,
succulent and measureable only by
sextants and the degrees
between them; this is not the
reason to print money
but to give it away-

to be honest, I earned my head today,
every ounce. the mice ran the kingdom.
the kingdom really only created mice.

I said while drowning in
your absence that the shell of
a crab is prettier than watching
the meat being sucked out of it,
but no one appreciates the ugly
for what they are:
important.

this is why they
can't stop printing money.

the seconds going by
like the people
on their way
to obscurity,

and the people going by
like seconds,
like little cruel
seconds,

when you cannot
accept being
alone.

if you need
to make a fire

I hear world peace
burns best of all,

but start with
the money

and stay away from
my dry
and unshaved
heart,

at least until
the sun goes
down and away.

It Seems Everyone Must Follow

those lands which ate my
father as he walked
towards a noise
he'd followed-

(the sweet singing of
mistakes and the small
little elations and orgasms
of new thoughts)

as he walked
through the air
like doors
that swung,

and disappeared,

as I stand here at
the same doors,

looking at
my little
girl
draw
for the last
time.

Always So Close
To Knowing

A Pig To 3 Pearls Ratio

"I've always felt
sorry for the generals of armies,
whether they
won or were
defeated," I said out of nowhere.
"you can't kill that
many people and
think you're doing
something that makes sense."

I looked at the mellowing wood window sill
cooking in the batter of the sun.

there was no real reason
for me to say that,
no one was having a conversation
that was even close,
and everyone who
was there looked at me
strange, as if I'd escaped
from a different dimension
and just learned earth's
mannerisms.

I looked at their smirks and replied,
"well, if war were so pretty
and wonderful, why'd we need two world wars?
if it were that beautiful wouldn't we have
stopped at one?"
before I got up
and went to the fridge.

"what the hell are you
talking about?"
said someone
who I didn't even know.

I raised myself from the chair, grunted.
I shrugged my shoulders.

"wisdom
can't wait for
the right crowd,
lady.

maybe
it's all supposed
to make sense
after it's
too late,"
I said.

"but I'm a man,"
they said.

I shrugged
my shoulders
again.

"that was
a compliment,
little lady,"
I said.

Lake Drained Of Peace

how's that job as a criminal and a sheriff
going for ya?

the slick streets combed back and
the women always something-

it'd be nice to remember
the things that can't remember
themselves, letting the black sky make
us equal when the blue sky couldn't,

being the meat and bone we mostly are
with a certain tuning to it,

the way things seem to go through
us like x-rays.

was our head ever ours?

your guess is as good as the rest of
these idiot's ideas.

each toilet
a shrine to shitting
into the water that
keeps us alive.

how's that job as a dead man
and a mortician working out for you?

get any hits?

do you deserved to be hit?

orange tree,
stuck in the middle of nowhere,

I speak to you, and only you,
though you cannot hear me:

I understand
what it's like to
give your fruit
to total strangers,

and I like how you
put it the other
night
as you
stuffed your
leaves
with dew,

pointing out
how mr. know it all
only had a single
window

and
how one
single view
can really
distort things.

Salvation Isn't A Bus Stop

some are still waiting
for the second coming.
even after all the shit
we've been through
with wars and
plagues and revolutions,
they think some big
show is still planned,
demons, angels, and all-
it is as if they think
Michelangelo and
Fellini never came.
as if they had never heard
of Monet or Rowling.
But they were here.
they were here
and so was Dali, Twain.
there was Harriet Tubman,
Lester Young, Hedy Lamarr,
and all those Gandhi's.
there was Lincoln,
Muhamad Ali, Kant,
Plato, Sexton,
Oppenheimer,
Mrs. Roosevelt,
Confucius.
Picasso's granddaughter,
Stieglitz, Hal Ashby,
and plenty of others
as good if not
different enough

to be better.
there were, and are,
those who came
that didn't need
saving that way.
that skipped the okay,
the blessings of the church,
and the approval of
the council.
these were self-created
kings and queens
who still tried
to uplift the cretins
of their times with art,
with love, with yelling
and iron, with law and
and revolution, with myth
and music,
with light and the contours
of a body, with math
that stretched out the door,
and words that couldn't be erased
once they were spoken.
we have had more than one messiah,
and continue to,
over and over again.
in fact we've had hundreds
of thousands, if not millions,
of second comings.
we didn't need a repeat of
the first savior
who split like a dad and
didn't want the responsibility.

we got Beethoven and Haydn,
we got Stieglitz and Adams.
we got people who did the work,
gave us the insight and the notes,
changed the bad things to good,
added fire where fire needed to be
and also where it didn't,
gave the images and words
that needed to be given,
gave the peace and the thoughts needed
to expand the universe,
gave their lives when
they had to, took them when they had to.
those who were so good
at what they did
they could not live in fear-
they could not live in fear
of their own god not loving them,
their own ideas, their own judgement,
who followed their own instructions
under penalty of a worse death,
those green doors down the lane
of the centuries that opened
to anyone who turned their handles,
the choices and bravery
that wouldn't get us killed
or ostracized
but accepted.

they were the ones who saved
themselves and us along with them-
saving us the way we needed to be saved-
that way we needed to be spared-

that way
we still do
and we always
will-

it's
just that we don't
need a messiah
to do it
anymore,

thank
god.

Sargasam

here I am thrusting
a giant head like a boulder
to the bottom of the bottomless pit,
saying think,
think about it-

I smell of flowers and whiskey
and loathing, but I can live
with that. if I can live with
a cat in heat I can live
with that.

but can anyone else?
should anyone else?

of course something
smaller than the universe
keeps winking at me
and I am getting sick of
thinking there is an answer…

but back to the flowers, the ones I smell like-
they stood like prisoners against the wall.
the sun denied them water.
I picked them up from the ground
and hugged meaning back into them.

I carried them off and
left them all at the door of a stranger-

that harmless nice gesture started a fight

between a man
and a woman
I did not know,

or so I was later told
by my conscience.

after that I walked until I
found my way to the bar café.

in the corner may have been
the smartest person ever
hunched over and writing.

I just went to the counter
and asked for water.

they said they didn't serve my kind there-

like the sun,
like the women,
like the future,
like the past.

when I asked who
their kind was
they just froze,

that head of theirs
going back and forth forever
until forever was gone,

as it thought and thought

a million things times
a million things,

until all
it could
answer
was

don't
get smart with
me,

and I replied
you have no idea
how hard it is
not to do the possible.

She Just Called

you've developed these countries in me-
highly spontaneous countries,
their rains so righteous they
slip silver into the palm
of the doorman called fog
and make him go away.
now that it's light,
I would say eat the damn thing,
sky and all. pay the widow back.
favors are bombs. don't take them.
twist the dials, pull back the cover.
what use is another dead man in heaven?
is god even lonelier than Hugh Heffner?
my eyes are not merchants.
I am not trying to buy you.
sing the will. be the will.
the masses will not believe
in anything until someone
sues them for it, but
anyone who gets rid of lakes
is an idiot.
anyone who kicks
the snow off of mountains
doesn't deserve a sip of water.
as my pappy would say
don't bother hollering
at your reflection
to leave you alone.
there is no way to change
a man who cannot accept
who they are.

don't bother with
brushing your ego.
good work
needs no feelings.
good work needs
no honors.
that is why I am
standing out here in
the morning with its light
pouring down on my
throbbing head
like rain,
dialing.
my dimes
are not for the boatman.
I just need to call Ellie
and tell her
she is not alone.

Whooping The Whole Place

looks of shock on their
genteel smoked fat bodies
having died like 10,000 skin cells
in one hand clap,
the lackeys rolled up like
coins for the bank,
a roll of black electrical tape
left on the table, the table without
a chance to get dusty,
tired of taking care of the beast
who looks to devour me,
a debt looking to enter my pockets,
but I have determined I will go
fighting and not in my sleep,
clearing the pool table of
threats and challenges,
standing alone and
leaning in with a pool cue,
left alone but curious
about what tomorrow will
look like after I beat
the hell out of it today,
having torn off a little piece of
that black tape
and made each loser wear it
on the way out
after I was done-
go ahead check; you see all those
people looking down?
I beat them.
I pulverized them.

I did what I was meant to do.
I never even had to
shoot a thing.
I just let their ego
take care of them
for me and lined up my shot.
I can't help but
think that's all
it will ever take
to defeat
anybody. or
didn't you know?

impossible is
just something
someone hasn't tried
yet.

If You Never Ask

with practice one can become
less than themselves,
dream others dreams,
starve to feed something else,
be thought for and not thought of.

one can gut themselves
completely
while leaving their guts
still inside them.

one can cover everything
in a nice lie,
the color of invisible, and
act as if death will
happen to anyone
who disagrees
or mentions otherwise.

one can do it so simply,

with little or no effort,

patriotically or
anarchistically.

it doesn't matter.

one can be someone
else more easily
than they can ever be

themselves.

truthfully,
even if you
have the courage
and the will and
the gall
and the smarts,

you still might
not be promoted
past patsy.

the only sure
way out of anything
is death,

so I don't
know what to
do for you

if you don't either,

and
if you're going
to sit there
with me telling
you this
like ghost stories
around a fire

we both
know

it may be
too late
as it is-

and so I wish
you the very
best

whomever
you've accepted
you are

and whatever
they've made
you out
to be.

I only want you
to understand I did not
disagree with you
so I could fight
you, hurt you,
or kill
you

but
just so I didn't die
as someone
I never
knew.

When The Only Person You Trust
Is The Doorman

Horatio's hat is in the water,
laying in a barbarians puddle,
the whole stinking mess
unpreventable because a damn
is a damn, and no matter what they say
you can't take back a scar, you can't undo
a cherry that got eaten,
you sit a man in the spark box
and he is gonna find
all that he has left to say inside him,
and when I sat down
to face you all I could say
is love hates me,
and I sat back and my spine curled
like a magazine about ready to swat
the stars buzzing around my
head, but you had a great response,
and I greatly appreciated it-
love hates everybody,
you said.

and with that
I poured one
for the great times
when nobody can
hear us laugh
or watch
us cry.

The Ignoring Of The Street Lights

the burning of many bodies
is never a good sign,
or did you forget the king
who was just here,
and the century now
that will never be?

our gods being less like
protectors and more like
voyeurs,

my own hand carving
my own eyes
to see what I am carving,

all those eternal
loops that come with heart
and heart breaking-

the whole damn
city thrown into
confusion

while it slides
out of the shell
and into the dark of
a giant throat,

with all those street
lights you
walk safely

home under

being
someone's
smoldering
loved one.

The Glass Of Water In The Fire

what do you call someone
who runs into a fire
to get a glass of water?

you could call them
an idiot, a fool.

perhaps desperate,
dangerous,
suicidal, even mother.

you could even call
them your friend,
whether it was true or not...

but for some reason
we never think
it will be us.

we are all prepared to think
we could never be so desperate,
dangerous, or suicidal.

that we think we have something
that would keep us out
of the fire instead of in it.

but the truth is
every day we walk into
the fire to get a glass of water.

every day we face death
a thousand ways,

even when we know
what we could be doing is killing
ourselves,

like dreaming of lost love,
holding onto things
that do not exist
like mimes.
driving at night.
flying to Denver.
returning for the knife.
even opening a door
for someone.

we can even do it
when chasing our dreams.

we endanger ourselves
all the time
whether we play it safe
or not.

we commit suicide
after suicide
in just telling
the truth to
those we may
never truly know.

but we do it anyway.

we have to do it anyway
if we want to stay sane.

and so we walk toward
the next house on fire
to get a glass of water.

we sit down
among the flames
at the table.

we sit there
and all we can do
is drink that glass of water
until it is gone, get up,
and then go find the
next place on fire.

all we can do is
look among the flames
for the reason we are here.

today I hope I
find a good one.

Playing A Gig At The Dining Room Table

it's about the most I can give birth to as a man-
being funny, here under the ashy
and caramelized moon-
the cloudy elephants having marched back over
the alps, taking with them many shadows.
perhaps it is not wonderful everywhere,
but I still think that's okay.
in fact I think it is more than okay
if I can make a joke about my face and
get the kitchen crowd going.
I'll be damned if the world makes
any more sense without agony
than it would without humor.
so if the rip in my pants can
get us out of hell, then by all means,
laugh the blimp laughter that floats
up above our heads among the stunt plane flies
and cigarette smoke ghosts,
each of us a giant something or other
doing very little, each of us related
to a graveyard stiff, each of us
the children of alcoholics and misfits,
prisoners, black sheep, armies that
never formed. we all need to be reminded
that even royalty had epileptics,
heretics, and sycophants in their halls.
it is good that with as little as we have
that we still act human on a summer night.
that when we sit in the dining room
of a small place on a summer night
there is nothing wrong with almost

pissing our pants about the time
Ben confused a gas can for a
water jug, or John tried to cheat
at checkers using an Oreo cookie,
or Elaine pooped her pants and
got caught trying to leave her underwear
at the back of the school bus.
it's more important that we laugh
than we cry, knowing we survived.
it's important we make fun of life,
throwing peanuts at each other,
pouring less than expensive drinks,
asking each other for lights and the time.
it's good that were laughing to keep
ourselves up,
making sure
the day is done
and not coming back,
laughing to keep
ourselves alive,
laughing to
prove you can
live without love.
laughing because
it's so fucking funny
how fucking sad
life really is
sitting around a table
with a bunch of
drunken idiots
with no
guts to assassinate
the president

they hate.

but then
who said
jokes have
to be funny.

Permanent And That's It

the unknown is permanent, and that's it-
consciousness being a thick lit candelabra
that shows us no more than
what's a few feet around us.

look, even the rain is scared of
its own thunder and lightning.
see it trying to claw through the windows?

that's not the act of something natural.
that's the act of something wild, scared.

in fact while you're here
here's a quick story about San Diego.
there were some soldiers stationed there long ago.
a woman was raped
but the wrong man was hung for it,

and if you'd been there
the only thing you would have been
was dead or guilty too
no matter how innocent you were.

that's what I mean by the act
of something wild, scared.

so lest the light of all these electric devices
burn out our passion for life,
lean over, turn everything off,

and listen to that new god raging in the sky.

listen to it kick all the water out of the sky.

you can't tell me while
we stand here soaking wet
in a doorway
that you saw it coming.

nobody see's the unknown coming.

it's permanent and that's it.

Gladys' Daughter And I

time just punched a man in the face
and ran off with his youth,
and oh the liquor stores
sing with ringing registers,
and every transaction is
a possible robbery.

Bobby says he has got smoother moves
than the whole regime of china,
and Marvin adds only if the whole
regime has diarrhea,
which causes Bobby to smack
him in the back of the head,

his cigarette falling
from behind his ear to the floor,
as everyone looks down
to find it but me.

see I am going to meet Marne
and we are going to go looking for cars
under the glow of the moon.

we're gonna see if we can
find a golden palomino
with the initials DJ
carved into the dash.

apparently that's the car
we're supposed to get back
for her mom Gladys,

● ● ●

though that's just what we tell Gladys
to get her off our backs
when we stay out drinking
rainwater and lemon.

she doesn't mind how we smell
when we come over
as long as she thinks we're still looking
for that car that got towed
away long ago,

the one that she drove Tom
crazy in, argued he could never park
it well or knew how to fix it,

that he didn't have the touch
to get the engine to turn.

in fact she drove him so crazy
he pretty much never left the road.

he's been out there so long
Tom probably broke his neck looking
at everyone he couldn't be
drive right on by,

and now he's paralyzed with fear
every time he tries to go home-

and what a broken heart to keep,
what a broken thing to be,

wandering
the valley of death
and
looking for a gas station
that still sells
champion oil

for a car that
isn't even there.

Humor Is Useful In Telling Hard Truths

maps won't find it, Charlie.
fate's not a fixed point
but a result. if you find love
you might be luckier than some.
if you don't find it
you might be luckier than us all.
it's a gamble either way,
the kind even emperors have taken.
cities have been lost over it,
centuries completely changed.
men and women both have
been driven mad by it.
tortured by it.
murdered and arrested for it.
the libraries of the world,
their museums, theaters,
temples, markets,
streets, are all filled,
stuffed to the ceilings,
with their results,

many of them
being as
unbelievable
and distorted
by their
creators as by
their viewers-

but my god
we'd be a pointless

creature
if we ever stopped.

if we just unloaded
all those works
and dumped them into the fire.

all we'd be is sane,

and what
fun would
that be

let alone
useful

when stuck in
Havana
under a fallen
regime.

Shade Of Red

there are some colors of red
that will never devastate me-
love, fire, blood, apple,
the dress that ended the war-

there are some places that
only exist when you close your eyes.

so close your eyes
and please take that idea,
that special red, into universe number 27,
and wander between the blades of swords and snow.

(the rumor is that there is only one universe
but I count more heads than that;
they also say thirteen is bad luck,
but I don't see it operating any differently than
any other number, after all I was thirteen once).

after that open your eyes to hide it there,
so the chicory can grow
after mourning the mothers
that never were
and the futures that
should have never been,

(which is an entirely different
color altogether).

leave it there to be
harvested

like feelings
in the skin.

even though
it matches
everything
dark you
could think

it will still
never
be the color
red that
I was thinking,

that I hid
in universe
27,

to create
the answer
for why
tigers
never marry
or
death
never says
I can't.

Preamble To The Mercenaries Handbook

what was it that mercy said again?
the thresher was too loud
and I was confused by the overuse of gold.
if there was a purpose I don't think I could
find fault in it, but
I don't think sitting at the front of the classroom
made any difference. honestly, I am not
sure there is a difference anymore
between suicide and honesty-
it kills us, it seems, no matter what.
yellow bowls don't offend me
but I've seen less make a woman pack.
as I said, Houston was supposed
to be a great place and look how
that turned out – a book that
ripped its own cover off
and let the flies take over.

I am suggesting you can find that important
if you want to,
but it shouldn't make you forget
that the small creatures
walking through the dust of giants
are just trying to live without being crushed.
let the rain water the plants.
Tuscany doesn't have to change its name.
bravery can be found in an ant
and everyone needs some kind of therapy.
but who can afford
that on the truth?

the vestige of a place that
has yet to be- burlap and
silk:

if these ideas
can share the world,
so can we,

and obviously I am calling your bluff
on saying you need the whole bed.

from what I can tell
the one armed knight
stands with his own sword
at his throat
right now.

it is the only way
he can tell you
the end of the story

about what
the most powerful
resort to

when they
cannot find
a challenge.

Regarding To Self-Loathing

what was god but something
that I thought was stronger than me
instead of as fallible as me,
instead of a clean dish
that would allow itself to be used,
needing the luck of the torn skirt Rita wore
as she ran out of the laughing man's office,
stuck in perpetuity
like the purple bruises which
lined the boy's back
as he laid in the grass
and thought of never going home.

the reality is that all are gods
changing their fates continually,
and whoever sent those flowers
to that secretary sure fucked
up my chances, but I say if
this is Thursday,
at least it's
not the last Thursday
that came through
in spurs with a mop,

declaring chaos be gone
when that's all that's kept
this place going,

as my adopted mother
can attest to

on her stolen bible
from the department
store

where
she used to
work
in returns.

Weigh A Little

some day
you will
weigh nothing.

some day you will
eat nothing,

breathe nothing.

someday everything
you know will go dark.

you can see
me now,
but someday
that will not be
possible.

some day
everything about you
will live at the mercy
of other's memories-

so
if you really
want to figure out
if this is all
worth it,

now would be
a better time

than a time
you will not
live to see.

do it
right now
while you have
the brain and eyes
and no guards
or bars
around your soul,
as spring takes off winter
and lets her trees grow wild.

look at life
not as something
to solve

but as something
that must prove its worth,
just as anything else.

existence itself
does not prove worth.

existence only proves
you are at the mercy of
entropy and ideas,

and since you
have the time
to read poetry

I would say now is
a good time to decide
if this reality,
to you,
is simply
a huge nothing
slathered in onions,
with everything
an endless
braying into
an endless void,

or if it's a
paradise
some don't even know
they are in because of
all the imperfections
that come with it.

now would be a good time
to see if it is
worth drinking
in the kitchen
alone as your
lover could be
who knows where
doing who knows what
with who knows whom.

see if sitting on
the couch is better
than being shot at in a war.

see if you can understand
the fire in a pit
or if you can admire
the art on a wall.

see if it's worth
writing down your ideas,
trying your hand at
fixing cars, or
surviving the swords
both real and imaginary.

see if you weigh something.

see if you've got the moxie,
the nerve, to run doubt out of town.

get a feel for the place.

realize that realization
enlarges your eyes
but not your chances,
and understand that you
may never understand,

but at least take the time
to know what you don't know.

have the guts to admit
what you are before you have no guts.

this is omega speaking to alpha,
this is a ghost speaking

confidentially to another ghost.

this is coming to terms
with the blood on the floor
and the blonde in the doorway-
the broken window, and
the scream in the other room.

this is reality saying
your life is the only response
you will ever have
to the question
of if you ever lived,

as you step outside
into the cold and shudder
a little internal quake,

to remind you of that thing
that fights inside you
no matter what you do,

that thing that
answers for your soul
before there is no more change,
before there is no more anything.

that little thing
inside of you
that says
now
is the only time.

Keep This First Line

the only escape is acceptance-
see what I have made in tears?
it is nothing. the universe
does not look at me. not out of shame.
I am too small to matter to it.
you are like the universe to me,
and I accept that.
the exploding joke cigar stars
going off all around this
dear old place.
the commonalities, the integers,
the whole damn thing
really just as indescribable
as ever. god is the only drunk
who might survive this accident,
but not the way god wanted,
for even a god can apparently
be forgotten- or a better way
to put it is to quit pretending-
for the rest is laid out in atoms.
everything is atoms.
even my memories.
even the fates I never had.
once you accept
that, well damn it,
break open the heart atoms
and let the champagne
atoms flow to the atom floor,
because now we can use
our love atoms
and celebrate how ridiculous

these atoms are,
acting like
they have never
even met
themselves.

Short Cut Through Olympus

pistons which operate
the jaw, words which
give it the work.
there are bridges in my badge,
my badge being my chest.
I am allowing things out of myself,
I am enforcing some
kind of belief,
some kind of lawlessness,
ideas bootlegged, sent under
tarps and pine,
crossed over the border,
passed prisoner to prisoner,
the mountains sitting on walls,
guarding deer and wolf,
nature is likely related to
big city thugs, it can't just stop
raining, we all know this,
probably got its manners from its
drunken father, abusive,
wearing a dirty cloud shirt,
making women of us all
with its thunder,
strong and tough women
with only the power to defy,
not deny, how hooked we are on
poison, sugar cane never even saw us coming-
and time- time still hoping to put
back together a cup by walking backwards,
love could become even more ridiculous
than hate if we aren't careful, if we're

just talking to talk and inventing roach spray
instead of tolerance, the distance
of my insides as infinite as they are finite,
those birds not flying anywhere
probably knowing more than science,
those hooded monks
standing near the fence refusing
to evolve anymore, letting me reclaim
the idea of a sober sea
that keeps polishing the shore
like the mane of a horse or the hood
of a car, we may be tiny little thieves,
unimportant and breakers of laws,
but we sure as shinola can sneak
some big ideas into the universe
when you need them,
some ideas so big that,
WOW,
even
your mother
can give birth to herself
after your-
WOAH-
father
got fixed.

Good Part Of The Story

the horse got away with dragging
Sal all the way out past Tallamussac.
I even marked the page. fake silver apples were
lined around a bowl in the hotel. it seemed like they
had no idea what hospitality was. I had to remember
though that I did not come for the fake apples,
the same way the horse did not take apples for
apologies after all the spurs Sal put into his side.
when it came time to sing, as you would
for anyone you want to leave, I did so in my head.
I cheered in fact, sitting in my underwear
in a chair that stuck to my back and thighs.
we must achieve victory somehow to stay alive,
even if it is only through fiction.

Thankful For What's There

most, not all, but most
   have been invented
      into a
         dependency,
wired to damn near
explode
if   the power
goes out, like out out,
like pop's never coming back and
    took up with that lady in Fresno-

playing the
knob game, trying
    to find some
fool worth listening to,
        until,
           until,
     wait-
no, forget it,

just clink these
glasses together-
it's hopeless and I hate
scrabble.

look, even the
pigeons are
damn near killing themselves
    for a ride out of reality,

can't even get a look from

a two year old-

Christ, it's nearly over
for us all-

        but isn't it always,
        isn't it always…

and yet someone always finds
a fiver somewhere,

someone   has a mom
      who cares,

gives nickels when
she has them,

a cure comes too late for some
and right on time for the rest,

there's no rhythm to that drum, I know,

but I got some apples,
        some of the best,

and we're not going
anywhere,

        like the boat to Spain
      we read about
awhile back,
resting firmly on the rocks,

remember? the men scrambled around
screaming
to be rescued

      but the waves were too tough,
           and the men just got knocked
off, one by one by three or two

          while everyone on shore
just stood there
watching as though
someone was just going
to change the channel,

and I don't know, maybe we're
the guys on the rocks, or maybe
we're the guys just watching,

      either way,

       I'll take matches and
          candles
     over worry
       any day.

Excursion

a man
bird watching
looked to his side and saw me.

he nodded,
as if I were okay with him,
as if it were okay I were there,
as if he had somehow knew me,
or at least knew what species
I was.

I asked him how many birds
he had seen in his life.

he said all but the dodo,
he said that was his goal.

even though we both knew
they were extinct,
I got it.

he needed something
he would never see
to keep going.

he smelled of pipe smoke,
had silver glasses, and looked
as though he were homeless
and had not
had sex for a long time.

he took a hit form a flask
and raised it to me.

no thanks I said.

he said you ever wonder
what this world would be like
if it didn't have birds.

I said less shit on my car,
more bored cats, and
hardly anything
to go with toast.

he laughed and said,
wish I'd met you long ago,
when I could still use friends.

I said how old are you?

he said 43. and you?

48, I said.

you look thirty, he said.

just then
my wife came from
around the corner.

I am ready to get the fuck out of here, she said.

well, I said, good to meet you.

good to meet you too, he said,
and then put his binoculars
back up to his face.

as we walked back to the lot
my wife was complaining
about her hips,
but as she was
I saw him again.

he got into a gold
Mercedes
and drove off.

he may still
be looking for
something
he will
never find,

but I actually think
he was my
dodo.

Sounds Like What It Is

say snow. it sounds like what it is,
but nicer. say my name. I didn't pick
my name, by the way. it sounds like something
that would eat leaves. I wonder why
someone thought I would eat leaves? maybe my
mother thought it sounded regal. maybe my father
didn't want to argue, thought I should be
named after a dead relative. maybe they both
thought I was preserving some line of DNA.
I don't really know what to think of my name
even though it is mine.
I like your name though.
it sounds like someone who would read books,
write in cursive, know the names of Greek gods.
the Greek gods have some pretty good names.
half of them must have been named after making
love. the other after getting drunk.
they may have even in some way named
themselves. after all
their statues look like they carved themselves,
I can't see why the gods couldn't have named
themselves. I don't see why I couldn't name myself
also. why I couldn't just go by Lorish Amplin.
maybe that isn't the point of names.
I could just say yes. yes sounds
like it's both good and bad. so does no, but no
always gets this bad rap. it scares other people,
makes them aware we aren't going
to just do what someone says.
that we are going to think about it,

maybe even disagree. it seems more people are
afraid to disagree about it than just not think
about it. more people built the coliseum than
designed it. more people come to look at the statue
of David than those that carved it.
maybe there are no seas left to discover here,
but somewhere I bet there is. I bet there
are other Neptunes, other incredible ideas.
I'll bet you there is even someone
you've never even heard of
slaving away in a room,
trying to finish some sentence.
trying to put the last touches of paint on a canvass,
not maybe even less than an hour away.
I'll bet you there's one even closer,
that there might even be something
better than the sun,
standing in a bathroom applying eye shadow,
something so powerful you can find men regretting
their names, trying to finish something
that explains why, but their never seems
to be enough paint,
there never seems to be enough time,
there never seems to be anything
other than this name we have
that no one can see until they give us
a tombstone, and even that may not say it.

While I Ponder The Failure Of Charms

tangled in lives,
in all the directions of time-
the physics alone suggests
rain in here means just as much
as it does out there.

villains? I've got plenty of those.

I have often sworn an oath
to someone who wore a different
face, a different morality,
and then they changed them
when they were bored,
and then I was promised
to someone and
something else
completely.

this kingdom is not kind.
it is brutal to the soul
that isn't there.

a loquat tree still grew
though. that was good.
I ate its fruit like soft jewels,
my glistening lips
enlivened. my betrayal
all but gone.

still it is unnerving.

that lake with
all those dead cats
in it, murdered just to
throw an entire population
off like that-
saying they were witches
just to hide one lie.
all that waste
to hide one lie.

I feel sorry for lovers
who only think they
will always love

who only know
how to love.

there is so much
more to love-

the world is
full of so many
dead things
already.

some days
I think
it'd be better
if people just
blew up when they
became useless

but then I guess

we'd all be dead,

which might
sound even
crazier after
I admit

I just wish
it were quiet
enough
tonight
that
all I heard
were explosions.

Movere

dogs pacing in the moonlight.

the ancient ruins left to rot in the jungle.

learn from your predecessors –
we do not eat if we just stand still.

we do not live if we just sit here.

we have to follow
the rain, the food.

when there is none
belief is not enough.

we must go and find it
wherever it is.

we must
leave the emptiness,
the lovelessness,
the rumors and the secrets.

we must give away
the familiarity,
the comfort of
inaction,
the predictability.

we must pack,
separate

from devastation,
be open to learning,
and admit when we are not wise
or when we are wrong.

we can retrieve ourselves
from the rubble of the evening.

we can remove
ourselves from
doubt, its claws
and its lies.

we do not have
to die in vain,
standing there
dry and starved.

we can go.

we can just pick a direction
and live.

we can live until
we can't believe
our own lives.

we can live until
we've lived
not one,
but several
good lives,
doing several

good things.

we can live until
flowers celebrate us.

we can live until
we are art.

we can live until we
are wine.

we can live until
even death
remembers us.

we can be more
than names.

we do not have to be understood.

we can be more than just understood.

we can move.

we can be told.

we can be lore.

we can be spoken.

we can live.

When A Bullet Shell Drops

cylindrical, that is how I see it,
imported from a dream like wine from another
country or dimension,
held up to the light to properly take in all sides,
finding out some sides are taken more than others,
as some never know what a childhood is
and others think they have found
the fountain of youth in immaturity,
my game of jacks never finished and
my last meal as good as anyone's guess,
the betting board full of odds but no forgiveness,
but to complete this circle:
the last time I saw my dog it was
the day before my ex decided
it was time for him to leave,
and I held that golden bastard,
I tore up the script and read straight from the
tears, trying to bless each word as it
left my mouth, like it were a reprieve from pain,
saying your life of all lives
was not in vain,
as his look left him
and his name left him and
supposedly they carried him out
in a black bag, so black that even now,
the old man that I am
and all the things I have been through,
knowing he would have been
dead by now anyway,
I will still say it was
too soon.

Consequence Within Consequence Within Consequence...

what has snow has a present, a now,
    and that allows me to be as much
        existence as possible;
it allows that snow to melt, to spend the day
    with a memory, call your
grandmother after death, even if you're
       only talking to yourself-

so of course there are limits, but
we have the essentials- roller coasters,
cliffs, a ballpark, ocean, jobs, etc. etc.-
but not everything on a round planet
has to be round.

    for example 450,000 years ago
is only long ago if you try to live there.

but when you're here you have people
to speak to, bottles to open, time to complicate,
    compliments to live down,
favorites to be outdone by other favorites,
surgeries to endure, aging bodies
to test the limits of love, laws to remove
from our sight.

what could have been a sure thing
turns into something better
when we can't
predict if it's a boy
or a girl or a

problem or an adventure
or an apology
or an experiment.

would it be better if stupidity never were?
would it be worse if I did my jail time
in a place that wasn't a jail?

why worry about being tested by Satan
when you've already met Martha,
been stuck downtown, or waited outside
an office?

I'm sorry, but if I pass you
the salt it's easy to ignore me after that,
so if you come back to me
it is because you want to.

if the joint is a dump
the only thing you can do
is make it a great dump to be in.

        remember, you smell with your brain and
not just your tongue.

remember that your memory is the most important
unimportant thing there is, and then
do the human thing
and forget it,

        and appreciate
at least one thing
everybody else hates,

and let the end
            make its changes,

for it sits everywhere constantly
        like a cigarette smoke,

and that is how april
warming the limbs of clouds
with its hands
            makes it a nurse,

        while the rain
types and types
and types throughout
            the night

to its blind brother
            snow

        about all the so many
            unpublished
flowers.

Spare Spare Time

enough has been crushed.

I stay the song
even after the voices
stop singing.

I participate.
I find the living.

I am no one's king and the world is better for it:

but do not send me thanks.

do not act as though
this is something incredible-

this is not an orange
growing in a tree.

this is not a fish willing
to swim into a net.

it's less than a bird.

I have seen far better summer days
accomplish more than an army.

don't be fooled-
I am just a human
trying to stay worthy
of being in their own body.

I lay bread on the plate
for those that deserve it.

I lay something else at the feet
of those that don't.

the future is only in two directions:

either out there or down inside.

I can't tell you where yours is.

I only know how to live.

I have no idea how to love.

perhaps that's why I'm still alive.

perhaps that is why I keep living.

Robert Benefiel is a North American writer and artist. He has written and created for over 30 years, in many different styles, and currently publishes under Poetastard Press.

Made in the USA
Middletown, DE
06 February 2021